D1414213

Party Games

For Kids

Fun Games for Classrooms, Church Groups and Parties

David T. Fox

Contents

Party Planner Guides

Selecting an 'It'

Many children's games have a special player referred to as "It". This player is given a special task such as selecting teammates or chasing other children. In other words, most kids will want to be It! Here are a few ideas on how to make that selection as fair as possible.

Rhymes

A rhyme can be used to help select who is going to be It. While saying the rhyme, go around the group pointing at a different child for each syllable. Whomever you are pointing to on the last syllable will either be It, or eliminated from selection, depending on the rhyme.

> "Engine, engine, number nine"
> "Going down Chicago line"
> "If the train falls off the track"
> "Do you want your money back?"
> {Pick yes or no)
> "N-O spells no, you don't get your money back"
> "Y-E-S spells yes and you shall have your money back"

> "Icka bicka soda cracker"
> "Icka bicka boo"
> "Icka bicka soda cracker"
> "Out goes YOU!"

"Blue shoe, blue shoe,"
"How old are you?"
(The child says their age which gets counted out)

"One potato, two potato, three potato, four."
"Five potato, six potato, seven potato, more."

"Eenie, meenie, meinie, moe"
"Catch a tiger by the toe"
"If he hollers let him go"
"Eenie, meenie, meinie, moe"

"Bubblegum bubblegum in a dish"
"How many pieces do you wish?"
(Pick a number and then count it out)

Pick the First or Last in Order

- Select the oldest/youngest
- Select the tallest/shortest
- Select the first/last birthday of the year
- Select the birthday closest to that day
- Select the first/last name alphabetically

Guess a Number

Pick a number between 1 and 20. Closest guess is It.

Lonely Farmer

30 Minutes

Room Size: Large, Outdoor

How to Play:

Select one child to be the lonely farmer who's missing his cows. The farmer will start the game at the "farm" which is any object or area that you select as the base. All the other children will be the cows who go missing. When the game starts, the farmer will close his eyes and count to 20. During this time, the cows will take off and find hiding places throughout the area. When the farmer finishes counting, he will head off looking for his cows. Since the cows don't want to get into trouble for leaving the farm, they must sneak back to the farm without getting caught by the farmer. Once they reach the farm, they are safe. If the farmer catches a cow before they reach the farm, that cow is It and will be the lonely farmer the next round. If nobody gets caught, the round ends when "all the cows come home".

Variations:

Don't let the cows have all the fun! Roosters, pigs, and horses like to play as well. For older kids, give the farmer a soft object to use to tag the cows as they return home. Better yet, hire a guard dog to keep watch as the cows come back. Anyone tagged by the guard dog must go back into the field and start again.

Four Corners

10 Minutes	**Room Size:** Medium

How to Play:

Choose one child to be It and have them stand in the center of the room. This child will close their eyes and begin counting aloud from 10...9...8... until they reach zero. During this time, all the other children will be quietly moving around the room, picking a corner in which to stand. When It gets to zero, without opening his/her eyes, that child will point to one of the four corners in the room and any children standing in that corner must return to their seats. The game continues until only one child remains. That child is the winner and can either be It the next round or they can choose a different child to be It.

Animal Noises

10 Minutes

Room Size: Small

Supplies Needed:
Paper or cards with animal names on them

How to Play:
Secretly hand each one of the children a card or piece of paper that has the name of an animal on it. For younger children, try using flash cards with pictures on them. Explain to them that when you say "Go!", they need to begin making the noise of the animal that they are holding. The children should then start walking around while trying to find other children assigned the same animal. When they find a match, they need to form a group and start looking for more animals of that type. When you see that all groups have been formed, call a stop to the game. To finish, have each of the groups take turns yelling out what animal they were.

Variations:
Turn this game into an icebreaker by replacing the animal cards with questions. For example, ask the children what

their favorite ice cream is or their favorite sport. The children then need to walk around and find other children that have the same interest.

Caterpillar Race

10 Minutes	**Room Size:** Medium

How to Play:

Split the children into teams of equal size so that each caterpillar will be the same length. You can have any number of caterpillars so having an odd number of children shouldn't affect it (although it may test your division skills). If there does end up being one extra child, they can be given the task of referee or cheerleader. After each team is formed, have the children think of a name for their caterpillar. The name should be short and easy to remember. Next, have each group line up with one child in front of the other. The children should place their hands on the shoulders of the team member in front of them forming a "caterpillar". Once the signal is given, the front team member will hop forward one step. The team member behind them will then hop one step and so on until the entire caterpillar has moved forward one step. Once the last team member has finished hopping, they shout out the name of their caterpillar. This lets the first child know they can hop again and the race continues. Keep going until one of the caterpillars reaches the goal.

Heads Up, Seven Up

| 10 Minutes | Room Size: Small |

How to Play:

Select up to seven kids to be It and come forward to the front of the room. There should be at least one child remaining in the group for each child selected to be It. To start the game, yell out "Heads down, thumbs up!" Each child remaining in the group must place their head down on their desk or lap and hold one hand in a fist with their thumb sticking up. While the children in the group are unable to see what's going on, the children who are It must go around and press down the thumb of one child. The challenge is to see who can be the sneakiest. Once all the children who are It have returned to the front of the class, yell out "Heads up, seven up!" (or "five up", etc.) Any child whose thumb was pressed needs to stand up and try to guess who pressed their thumb. If they are right, they get to trade places with the child who was It and the game starts all over.

Continuum

Room Size: Small

How to Play:

Divide the group into teams of 5 - 8 children each. Explain to the children that when you call out a topic, the children must arrange themselves in a line according to that topic. If you were to call out "age", the children must quickly form a line in order of their ages. The youngest will be on one end and the oldest on the other. If you called out "height", the children must quickly form a line from shortest to tallest. The goal is to have your team form the line in the correct order before any of the other teams. Whichever team is first (and correct), wins!

Suggestions for shout outs:
- Month of their birthday
- Number of pets they have
- Age / Height / Names in alphabetical order
- Favorite color/shirt color in order of the rainbow
- Number of siblings
- Time they woke up this morning

Human Knot

<table>
<tr><td>**10**
Minutes</td><td>**Room Size:** Small</td></tr>
</table>

How to Play:

Have the entire group of children stand in a circle facing each other. Each of the children should reach out their left hand and grab a hold of another child's hand. Once all hands have been connected, the children should reach out their right hand to grab a different child's hand. If it becomes too difficult for them to hold hands, you may need to break into multiple circles. When all the children have been connected, they must slowly begin to unwind the massive human knot that they've become. This will require twisting, crawling, walking through hoops of arms, and more! But remember, they cannot let go of each others' hands at any time.

Variations:

When playing with a larger group, try splitting the group into multiple teams to compete in a speed drill. See who can get untangled the fastest -- boys or girls!

Simon Says

10 Minutes

Room Size: Small

How to Play:

One child is chosen to be "Simon" and gets to stand in the front of the room. All the other children must stand an arm's width apart and should be facing Simon. Once the game starts, Simon will then call out an action for the other children to perform. If Simon starts the sentence with "Simon says...", then the children must perform the action. If Simon doesn't start with "Simon says..." then the children should not perform the action. Any child that performs an action when they shouldn't or doesn't perform an action when they should, must sit down. The last child standing is the winner and gets to be Simon in the next round.

Sample actions for Simon to call out:

- Hop on one foot
- Spin in place
- Rub your belly
- Make a funny face
- Wave to a friend
- Ribbit like a frog
- Say your name
- Touch your toes
- Cluck like a chicken
- Sing a song

Popcorn

15
Minutes

Room Size: Large

How to Play:

In an open area, have the children move around in a large group. They can be walking, dancing, skipping, or whatever it takes to keep them moving. After a few seconds, the leader will yell out a number and the name of an object. The children will stop moving around and form groups the size of the number. Each group will then attempt to form the shape of the object using their bodies. For example, if the leader yells out "Three Table", the children will form groups of three and attempt to form a table with their arms and legs. Once all the groups have formed their object, or at least tried very hard to, the children can go back to moving around the room in order to mix up the teams.

Variations:

For smaller groups, skip the moving around and go straight to creating small groups of two or three children. Once the leader has yelled out a number and object, the teams will race to see which team can complete their object first.

Sample Objects:

- Table
- House
- Tree
- Car
- Bird
- Ocean Waves
- Toaster
- Bike
- Surfboard
- Elephant
- Train
- Kite
- Merry-go-round
- Campfire
- Firework
- Worm
- Carwash
- Flowers
- Airplane
- Clock
- Bridge
- Crane
- Umbrella
- Ladder
- Gelatin
- Volcano

Who am I?

15 Minutes

Room Size: Medium

Supplies Needed:
Sheets of paper, Tape, Pen/Pencil, Scissors (optional)

How to Play:
Prepare the game by folding each sheet of paper into fourths and cutting (or tearing) along the folds. On each section of paper, write the name of an object, place, or person. Next, tape one of the pieces of paper to each child's back so they cannot see the word written on it. The children must then walk around the room asking each other Yes or No questions in order to get clues about the word on their back. Once the child is able to correctly guess the word written on their back, they can receive another word and join back in the game.

Variations:
If the children are too young to read, you can use pictures of objects instead. Try to keep the pictures simple and within a similar category such as sports, shapes, or animals.

Tag

15
Minutes

Room Size: Large, Outdoor

How to Play:
Start by gathering the children into a large open space and select a child who would like to be It. Once the game begins, whoever is It starts chasing the other children until they tag another with their hand. Depending on the variation of the game, that child is either It or is stuck until another child frees them. The game ends when all the children have been frozen or are It. If a game is lasting too long because the children are being freed too fast, start a new round with a different child being It.

Variations

Freeze Tag – Tagged children are frozen until freed by another child. The frozen child must hold the pose they were in when tagged. This can get hilarious!

Safe Zones – It can be fun to designate special zones within the play area as "bases" or safe zones. Kids that are within the safe zone or touching the safe object cannot be tagged by the child who's It. For fun, try making the safe zone a certain color or hard to reach area. Better yet, make the safe zone one of the adult helpers in the group!

Toilet Tag - If you get tagged, you become a toilet! Squat with your hand extended like a flusher until someone comes by and "flushes" you. (Sound effects are optional)

Chain Tag – Two kids are selected as It and must hold hands forming a chain. If a child gets tagged, they join hands with It and are now part of the chain. Once there are four kids in the chain, the chains breaks in half to form two groups of two kids. This keeps on going until everyone is part of a chain.

Blob Tag – When a child gets tagged, they join hands with It and become part of the blob. This continues until everyone is part of the blob. The last kid swallowed by the blob is It for the next round.

Tunnel Tag – Kids that get tagged have to stand in place until another child crawls through their legs to free them.

Vegetable or Fruit Tag – In this version, kids are able to protect themselves from It by squatting down and saying the name of a fruit or vegetable (or whatever theme you're going with).

Band-Aid Tag – After getting tagged, the child needs to place a hand on the spot that he or she was tagged. This is their "Band-Aid" and it must stay on for the rest of the game. If the child gets tagged a second time, the other hand also becomes a Band-Aid and must stay on the spot they were tagged. Once the child has been tagged three times, they must go to the "hospital" which can be any type of safe zone (or person!). After visiting the hospital, the child can rejoin the game completely healed!

Everyone's It! - Just shout this for the final round and see what happens!

500

20
Minutes

Room Size: Gigantic!

Supplies Needed:
Kickball or Football

How to Play:
Select one volunteer to be the kicker (or thrower) for the first round. The kicker will then stand on one side of the play area with all the other children spread out on the other end of the play area. The kicker then yells out a number between 50 and 500 right before kicking the ball into the air above the group of children. Whoever catches the ball gets the number of points shouted out by the kicker. Once a child reaches 500 points, they are the new kicker and the game starts over. If the ball hits the ground first, no points are given.

Tip:
Shouting out even numbers such as 100, 200, or 300 make keeping track of score a lot easier. However, older kids may enjoy other numbers like 25 or 500!

Snakes in the Gutter

20
Minutes

Room Size: Large, Outdoor

How to Play:

Pick two to four kids to be the "snakes" in the gutter. They'll need to line up in the middle of the play area to start. All the other children start out on the side of the playing area away from the snakes. Once someone yells, "Snakes in the Gutter!", the children along the side of the play area attempt to run through the gutter without being tagged by a snake. Any kids that are tagged now become part of the snake and must remain in the middle. Continue this until all kids have been tagged and are part of the snake.

Variations:

After a few rounds of the game, it can be fun to mix things up by changing how the kids run through the gutter. An example would be having everyone hop on one foot or even linking arms with another child. The variety will keep the game exciting for the kids.

Obstacle Course

| 25 Minutes | **Room Size:** Medium |

Supplies Needed:

Large variety of obstacles, Stop watch

How to Play:

Locate a variety of items around the area that can be used as obstacles the kids will need to crawl under, hop over, perform, or run around. Place these items in the shape of a track so that the children will know where to go. Once the obstacle course is assembled, time each of the kids as they run through the course to see who can get the fastest time.

Obstacle Ideas

Crawl Under/Through:

- Chairs
- Furniture
- Ropes (think limbo...)
- Tables
- Cardboard Box

Hop Over:
- Pillows
- Baseball Bat

Perform:
- Shoot Basket
- Jumping Jacks
- Push Ups
- Sing

Run Around:
- Cones
- Other Children

Variations:

For larger groups, try turning it into a relay race where the whole team tries to set a speed record. Relays can either have one or all kids running at once! This becomes an excellent way for kids to burn off some extra energy.

Capture the Flag

<table>
<tr><td>

30
Minutes

</td><td>

Room Size: Large, Outdoor

</td></tr>
</table>

Supplies:
Two "flags" or any object a child can easily carry

How to Play:
Select two bases on opposite sides of a large playing area such as a gym or field. Each base should have a "flag" (which can be any object) and a "jail". Next, split the children into two equal teams and have them stand by their bases. When the game starts, the children will run to the other side of the play area and try to grab the other team's flag. They must then return back to their base holding the flag and without getting caught. If they get tagged by the other team while trying to capture the flag, they need to hand the flag back and go sit in the other team's jail. The child must remain in jail until a team member from their side can tag them and set them free. The game continues until one of the children safely returns the other team's flag to their own base.

Strategies:

If playing with younger children, it may be helpful to give them a few strategies for playing the game. For example, it's a good idea to split up the roles within each team. Instead of having every child running towards the flag, designate some as "runners" and some as "protectors". The runners can charge across the field to capture the flag while the protectors can tag the other team's players as they come over. For added defense, try assigning some "prison guards" to watch over the jails. This will protect against the other team's players from being set free.

Name Game

Room Size: Small

How to Play:

Have the children sit in a circle on the floor. Ask each child to think of a word that starts with the same letter as their first name. The child can pick whatever they want but usually will end up with names like Brave Ben or Electric Ellie. Once everyone has selected their name, the leader will start by saying their special name. The child on the left of the leader will then say their special name, along with the leader's special name. Keep going around the circle with each child saying their special name, along with the names of those that have already gone. If anyone needs a little help, the group can give clues to help them remember. This game is a great way for a new group to get to know each other better and maybe learn something silly about their new friend!

What Time Is It, Mister Fox?

15 Minutes	**Room Size:** Medium

How to Play:

Have all of the kids line up at one end of the room. Select one of the children to be "Mister Fox" and have that child stand at the opposite end of the room. Mister Fox will be facing away from the rest of the children. To start the game, the children that are lined up will all yell out, "What time is it Mister Fox?" Mister Fox will respond by saying the hour. For example, "It's 3 'o clock". The children will then count out their steps towards Mister Fox up to the hour of the day. "1...2...3..." This repeats until the children are close enough to Mister Fox that he responds, "It's lunch time!" At that point, Mister Fox turns around and tries to tag one of the fleeing children. Whoever is caught gets to be Mister Fox the next round.

Variations:

It doesn't have to be "Mister Fox". You can use "Mrs. Fox" or any other name you can think of. Try picking the name of one of the adults in the group. Or maybe a familiar cartoon character.   Switching it up will keep the game entertaining for the children.

Mister Fox can also yell out "It's time to hop!"   All the children will start hopping their way towards Mister Fox until he says "Lunch Time!"   Other ideas could be skipping, crawling, or walking backwards.

Bug Hunt

<table>
<tr><td>**30**
Minutes</td><td>**Room Size:** Building, Outdoor</td></tr>
</table>

Supplies:

Plastic toy bugs from the dollar store

How to Play:

Before the children arrive or while they are distracted with an activity, the leader should hide an assortment of plastic toy bugs around the house, the building, or outside. When the leader says "Go!", the children race around the game area trying to find as many bugs as they can. The leader can assign a set time for the bug hunt or the children can play until all bugs are found.

Variations

- Assign different point values to each type of bug (beetle – 1 point, snake – 2 points, ladybug – 5 points)
- Play at night with flashlights only. This makes it harder to find the bugs and lets the kids try and sneak up on each other.

- Hide special "superbugs". These rare finds can be worth 25 points, candy, or special privileges such as selecting the movie to watch that night.

Battle Bug Hunt:

Make it a battle! If one player gets hit, tagged, or sprayed they have to set down their captured bugs for the other player to steal. This keeps the players watching out for each other in addition to searching for bugs. The more bugs a child is carrying, the bigger target they become!

Battle Types

Army Tactics – Equip the children with foam darts or balls they can aim at each other. Stealth and a good aim are key to victory!

Tag – A player must tag another player to capture their bug collection. May the fastest warrior win!

Water Battle – Getting another player drenched is the winning strategy here. Anyone who gets sprayed with water or hit by a water balloon has to drop their collection of bugs.

Doggy, Doggy, Where's Your Bone?

10
Minutes

Room Size: Small

Supplies:
Something small enough to carry in a hand

How to Play:
The game starts with one child being chosen as the "dog". That player must sit in front of the other children with their back facing them. The child playing the dog must then close his/her eyes while the adult places a small object behind the child. This object is the dog's "bone". With the room totally quiet, select one of the children in the larger group to sneak up and take the dog's bone without making a sound. Once the child has taken the bone, have all the children in the group repeat, "Doggy, doggy, where's your bone? Somebody took it from your home." The "dog" then tries to guess who took his bone. If the child guesses correctly, he gets to be the dog again. If not, the child that took the bone gets to be the next dog. Keep playing until each of the children has had a chance to be the dog.

Relay Races

15 Minutes	Room Size: Medium

Supplies:

Depends on relay

How to Play:

Split the children into two or more teams depending on the size of the group. Teams of 4 – 6 kids works great for most relays since the amount of time each child has to wait is minimal. Once the teams have been selected, have each of the children form a line for their team. Each of the lines should begin on the same mark, similar to runners lining up for a race. When all teams are ready, explain to them the rules of the relay you've chosen. Finally, say "On your marks...get set...go!" and watch them run. The first team to have all of their members finish the challenge, wins!

Relay Ideas

Running – The classic relay, kids need to run across the room to a specific target, tag it, and run back.

Hands and Feet – Walking on all fours, each child needs to make their way to the target and back.

Crab Walk – Using both hands and feet to walk but the child is facing upward so their back faces the ground.

Baton – The children run with a baton and pass it to the child at the other end of the relay. If they drop it while running, they need to start over.

Skipping – The children must skip their way from one side of the relay to the other.

Wheelbarrow – Two children partner up. The first child places their hands on the ground while the second child grabs their feet. The pair then walks down the field just like pushing a wheelbarrow.

Carrying an Object – Each child carries an object like an egg on a spoon or a water balloon on their head. The team with the least amount of broken eggs or balloons wins!

Hopping on one foot – It doesn't matter which foot, but each child must hop their way down field using only one foot.

Nose Push – Each child needs to place an object on the ground and push it across the room using their nose. Works best with balls or eggs.

Pass Along – In this relay, each child remains in their spot but needs to pass along an object from one end of their line to the other. For added silliness, allow the children to only use their elbows or knees.

Crazy Dress Up – Each child races back and forth between the two targets grabbing a piece of clothing from the pile and putting it on before running back. Sombreros, scuba gear, capes, boxing gloves, and feathered boas all make great props in this hilarious relay!

Sardines

45 Minutes

Room Size: Building, House

How to Play:

The ultimate hide-and-go-seek game, this is perfect for parties, lock-ins, and special events. Start by having all the kids gathered in one room. From there, send out one kid to go and find a hiding spot in another room. Have all the remaining children count out loud to 30 and then go running out to find the hiding child. Once one of the kids finds the hiding child, they are to *quietly* join them in their hiding spot. When another child finds the two hiding children, then *that* child joins the first two. Keep this up until there's only one child left looking for the hiding kids. At this point, it should be pretty easy since the group of kids will be packed together like sardines and giggling, wiggling, and pretty much making a lot of noise! The last child to find the group of kids gets to hide in the next round.

Tip:

Having adult helpers walk around during play will help younger kids who may need clues or directions.

I Spy...

How to Play:

Select one child to start the game and be It. That child will look around the room and find one object that the other kids will need to try and guess. The child who's It will then begin to describe the object by offering one clue at at time while saying the following rhyme.

"I spy with my little eye..."
"Something that is green!"

The other children can take turns guessing what the object is but after a few guesses, It should offer another clue. Clues can be colors, sizes, textures, anything! Keep offering more clues until one of the children guess what the object is. That child will then be It and can select a new object to "spy".

Giants, Wizards, and Elves

15 Minutes	**Room Size:** Large

How to Play:

This game is like real-life rock, papers, and scissors. Start by splitting the group into two teams. Each team then huddles together to pick what they will be this round – a giant, wizard, or elf. Once both teams have decided, all the children line up in the center of the room facing the opposing team. On the count of three, each team will yell out the character they selected.

Giants beat wizards
Wizards beat elves
Elves beat Giants

The team with the losing character then runs back to their base while avoiding being tagged by the other team. Any players who are tagged end up joining the other team. Keep playing until all players are on the same team.

Variations:

To get even more involvement, have the children act out their character while yelling the name. Silly faces always help too!

Red Rover

20 Minutes

Room Size: Giant, Outdoor

How to Play:

The leader forms two teams of children with an equal amount of older and younger children on each team. Each of the teams line up on opposite ends of the room and hold hands to form a wall. The team going first selects one child from the other team to call out. The team then yells out, "Red Rover, Red Rover, send <child's name> on over!" The selected child will then break free from his or her group and go running towards the other team's wall. If the child is successful in breaking through a part of the wall, the child is safe and can go back to his or her team. If the child is unsuccessful in breaking through the wall, that child will then be captured and will join the opposing team. The game ends when all children are on one team.

Two Extremes

How to Play:

Gather all the kids into the center of the room. Explain to them that you will be calling out two "extremes" or opposite things. After hearing the two extremes, they will need to run either to the left (for the first extreme) or to the right (for the second extreme) depending on which extreme they like the most. For example, if you called out "cake" and "cheeseburger", kids preferring cake would run to the left side of the room and the kids preferring a cheeseburger would run to the right side of the room. Repeat the game several times with each set of extremes getting sillier than the rest.

Variations:

If the room is small or you're just looking for variety, try having the kids perform an action instead of running to the side of the room. Have the first group hop on one foot while the second group does a cartwheel. Other actions include patting your head while rubbing your belly, running in place, curling up into a ball, or jumping jacks. The crazier the better!

Example Extremes:

- Pepsi / Coke
- Xbox / Wii
- Dog / Cat
- Winter / Summer
- Beach / Park
- Kleenex / Shirt
- Music / TV
- Football / Baseball
- Math / Reading
- Singing / Dancing
- Shoes / Sandals

I Didn't Catch Your Name

10
Minutes

Room Size: Small

Supplies:

Ball

How to Play:

Have the kids stand in a circle around the room while facing inwards towards the center of the circle. One of the children will be given a ball and will need to pass the ball to another child while saying their own name. The child catching the ball will then pass the ball to another child while saying their own name. This continues until every child has had the chance to say their name a few times. It's a quick, simple way to encourage the children to learn each other's names.

Variations:

The key to getting kids excited about this game is to use several different variations to keep it interesting. Instead of a regular ball, try using a beach ball, or a stuffed animal, or better yet, one of those gross, squishy toy balls with tentacles and lights! Another variation can be having the children say not only their name, but the previous child's name as well. For a real challenge, have the child catching the ball say the name of the child on his/her left or right.

Red Light, Green Light

| 5 Minutes | **Room Size:** Large |

How to Play:

Have all the children line up at one end of the room and select a volunteer to be the stoplight. The stoplight will stand at the other end of the room facing the line of children. To start, the stoplight will yell out "Green Light!" and all the kids lined up will start running towards the stoplight. After a second or two, the stoplight will spin around and yell out "Red Light!" Then all the kids running forward will need to stop immediately. Anyone caught moving after the red light has been shouted out will have to move back to the starting position. Keep alternating between green lights and red lights until one of the children reaches the stoplight and tags them. That child will be the stoplight the next round.

The Toaster Game

20 Minutes	Room Size: Small

Supplies:

Bread, Toppings, Toaster, Extension Cord, Ball

How to Play:

Place a toaster in the middle of the room and gather all the kids around it in a circle. Put a piece of bread in the toaster to start toasting it. This will be the timer. While the bread is in the toaster, begin passing a ball (or other object) around the circle. Whoever is holding the ball when the toast pops up must eat the toast with whatever mystery topping you have planned. Toppings could include chocolate, jam, bananas, ice cream, pickles, marshmallows...anything! Just be careful of any allergies (i.e. peanuts) the kids may have. Additionally, some children may not want to eat the mystery topping once they see what it is. If any of the children feel uncomfortable with the challenge, let them select another child from the group that is willing to try.

Variations:

In a normal game, the leader will have the toppings planned out in the order they want them to appear (i.e. save the best for last!). As an alternative, the leader can place each of the mystery toppings in a bag. The child holding the ball will then select their topping by closing their eyes and reaching into the bag. Whatever topping they pull out, they eat! Another variation, which is great if they know each other well, is to have another child select the topping. Place each of the toppings out on display for the kids to see. When a child is caught holding the ball, have either the child on their left or right select from the available toppings for them to eat.

Tossed About

25
Minutes

Room Size: Small

Supplies:
Box, Ball

How to Play:
Place an empty box in the middle of an open area. Explain to the children the goal of the game is to throw the ball so that it lands in the box without bouncing out. At varying distances from the box, identify several locations from which the kids will attempt to throw the ball. These can be identified by objects in the room (chair, door, etc.) or by putting a piece of masking tape on the floor. Inform the children of the order in which they should progress through the course. For example, the chair could be the first location. Once the child makes a basket at that location, they move on to the door next. There can be any number of locations depending on how long you want to play. Try to have a variety of easy and hard locations so that younger children will not get discouraged. Once the rules have been discussed, line the children up at the first location and begin

the game. If the child makes a basket, they can move to the next location. If the child misses or the ball bounces out, the child can go to the end of the line and wait for another chance. Keep playing until the children have conquered all stations.

Variations:
Try replacing the ball with a stuffed animal, or a bean bag, or a Frisbee, or candy! If using candy, reward the children as they complete each station. Another way to play this game is to use it for learning. At each station, have the child read or recite something before they throw the ball. You could also ask math problems or trivia questions as well. For churches, try assigning each station a word from that lesson's memory verse. At the last station, the child will need to recite the entire verse before winning.

Birthday Bash

10 Minutes

Room Size: Small

How to Play:

Place chairs in a circle with all but one child having a place to sit. The child without a chair will be It and will start calling out a month of the year. All children in the circle with a birthday that month will need to stand up and swap seats with another child that's standing. The child who's It will then try to sit in one of the empty seats while the children are switching chairs. If there's only one child with a birthday that month, that child will switch spots with whoever's It. For added fun, It can call out "Birthday Bash!" and all children will need to stand up and find a new seat.

Variations:

The kids can try calling out more than one month at a time. Any kids with birthdays during those months will all need to stand up and find a new seat.

Grab the Finger

5
Minutes

Room Size: Small

How to Play:

Have the children sit in a circle on the floor with their arms reached out on both sides. With their left hand, they should hold it open with their palm facing up. Their right hand should be in a fist with the "pointer" finger facing down. Their finger should be touching the center of their neighbor's opened palm. Explain to the kids that when you shout "Go!", they need to try to grab their neighbor's finger with their left hand while avoiding getting caught by the neighbor on their right. Any children with their fingers "captured" should sit out the next round. The game continues until there is only one child remaining.

Variations:

Try adding suspense to the game by using different words other than "Go!". For example, if you say "Green Light!" the children should try to grab their neighbor's finger but if you say "Red Light!", they should not. This way, the children never know if they should be on guard or not. For older children, try adding a rule that if they grab a finger on "Red Light!", then they must sit out. Another way to play the game is to mix up the pattern of open and closed hands. Try selecting a few children to have both hands open or both hands closed (with fingers pointing). Or try alternating the left and right hands by having the right hand open and the left hand closed. Change it each round to see which kids can remember the hand they're supposed to move.

"Have You Ever?..."

Room Size: Small

Supplies Needed:

A printed copy of the list for each child, Pencils

How to Play:

Prior to starting the game, type up a list of interesting questions the children can ask each other. The sillier the questions, the better! Hand out a copy of the questions to each of the children along with a pen or pencil. When the leader gives the signal, the children are to walk around the room with their list trying to find children who have done one of the items on the list. When they find a child who has, they write that child's name next to the item. The list can contain hobbies, sports, hair color, age, favorite color, or really anything! The goal is to get the kids interacting and learning more about each other.

Sample Questions:

- Favorite color is green
- Has a birthday in January
- Has been to another state
- Plays the piano
- Has a brother
- Is age 8
- Has been to a farm
- Likes spaghetti
- Owns a cat
- Can ride a skateboard
- Is missing a tooth
- Has a silly nickname
- Loves to dance

Charades

20 Minutes

Room Size: Small

Supplies:

A list of actions or characters to act out

How to Play:

Select a volunteer to come up in front of the group. All other children will need to be sitting so they can see the volunteer. Secretly show the action/character to the volunteer or if they cannot read, whisper it to them quietly. The volunteer then has to act out the action or mimic the character until the other children can guess who or what it is. Whichever child guesses correctly gets to be the actor for the next round.

Variations:

Depending on the age level, you can have rules such as "no making noise at all" or "just sound effects". The less noise they can make, the harder it is!

Back to Back

10 Minutes

Room Size: Small

How to Play:

Have each of the kids gather together in groups of two. If there are an odd number of children playing, one of the groups can have three members. Once the children are in groups, have them sit on the floor with their backs facing each other and elbows linked together. Tell the kids that on the count of three, they'll need to stand up by working together as a team. Remind them that their arms needs to remain linked at all times. Then count 1, 2, 3!...and watch the fun begin!

Variations:

This game works great for races and relays. Award points for the team that stands up first or turn it into a relay by having the kids first stand up, then walk to another area of the room. For added challenge, have the kids try and carry an object such as a stuffed animal or piece of candy (makes a great reward!). Turning the challenge into a tournament can be fun too. Another option is to see if the kids can stand up when there are three, or four, or five, or ten kids in the group! Keep combining the groups until the entire class is involved.

The best part of this game is that it can be used as part of a lesson on teamwork or cooperation. Try having one pair of kids demonstrate the challenge in front of the class. Then explain to the class how both children needed to work together to reach their goal.

Seltzer Shoot Out

10
Minutes

Room Size: Medium

Supplies Needed:
Box of Alka-Seltzer tablets, Double-sided tape, Water guns, Swim goggles (for duels)

How to Play (Group Mode):
Prepare for the game by taping or fastening an Alka-Seltzer tablet to each of the children's arms. Double-sided tape or duct tape turned inside out would both work. Make sure the Alka-Seltzer tablet is on the outside of the arm and is highly visible. These will be the targets the other children will be aiming for. Next, give each of the children a water gun and have them find a starting location away from each other. When the whistle blows, each of the children will run around trying to squirt the other children's tablets with water. Once hit, the Alka-Seltzer tablets will begin to fizz and eventually dissolve completely. The winner of the game is the last child with a tablet intact. For added fun, have the children who got out spray down the winning child in a final shower of water.

Variations:

Try grouping the children into two or more teams. Last team standing wins! To extend the game, try giving each child two, three, or five Alka-Seltzer tablets. The child can keep playing as long as one of the tablets remains.

How to Play (Duel Mode):

Pick two children to come up to the front of the room to get ready. They will each need a pair of swim goggles, an Alka-Seltzer tablet taped to their forehead, and possibly several towels. Once the children are ready, hand each one of them a water gun. On the count of three, each child will begin squirting the other child's tablet to get it to dissolve. Meanwhile, their own tablet will begin fizzing and foaming all over the place making the challenge harder. The first child to completely dissolve the other child's tablet is the winner!

Hand Squeeze Race

15
Minutes

Room Size: Medium

Supplies Needed:
Coin, Toy

How to Play:
Split the group into two teams and have each team form a line facing the other team. Once the children are lined up, have them hold hands with their teammates and close their eyes. At one end of the line, there will be a captain; one for each team. At the other end of the line, there will be a runner; one for each team. A few feet from the runners, place a toy (the crazier the better!) on the floor. When the coin is flipped, the captains (who can open their eyes) will watch to see which side of the coin lands facing up. If it's tails, they do nothing. If it's heads, they squeeze the hand of the teammate next to them. That teammate then squeezes the hand of the teammate next to them and it continues all the way down the line until it reaches the runner. Once the runner's hand is squeezed, they need to quickly get up and run to the toy you placed on the floor. The first team to

capture the toy wins and gets to rotate their players down one space. If the captain accidentally squeezed their hand after the coin landed tails side up, that team loses the round and rotates their players in the opposite direction. If playing with a small group, keep playing until one team cycles through all their players.

Variations:
Instead of flipping a coin, try asking a trivia question to test the children's knowledge. They can squeeze hands for "Yes" and do nothing for "No".

Piggy Wants a Signal

| **30** Minutes | **Room Size:** Building, House |

How to Play:

Begin by selecting a space or object to be the base. All the children will gather at the base at the start of each game. Select one of the children to be It and let the others know they will be hiding. The child who's It should close their eyes and begin counting to 20. While this is happening, all the other children should run and find a hiding spot in the building. When It gets to 20, they should begin searching for the other children. To help find them, whenever It calls out "Piggy wants a signal", all the hiding children need to oink from the location they're at. After oinking, if a child wants to move to a new location, they are free to do so. However, they must avoid getting caught while doing so. Whenever It finds a child, that child must return to the base and wait for the others. Once all the children have been found, the game is over and a new It is chosen.

Party Planner Guides!

The following pages are full of guides to help plan any type of children's party. From a sleepover with a few friends, to a large children's event, the party planner guides will help keep the party fun and exciting for the kids!

Quick and Easy Games
No set up and no supplies needed. These are perfect for filling gaps between activities.

Silly Games
Going for something memorable? These games are sure to make a mess and create memories the kids will cherish a long time.

Icebreaker Games
Great for new or shy groups looking for a game to get the conversations going.

High Energy Games
Active kids will love these games as they run and jump and burn off that extra energy!

Sleepover Games

Some games just work better at night. Try these
at your next overnight event to make a
long night into a memorable one.

Large Group Games

These games will keep the attention of the group
and keep the chaos to a minimum.

Quick and Easy Games

Party Planner Guide

Tips:

Always have one or two of these games ready to go as a backup plan. You never know when you'll need to fill an extra few minutes of time at the end of a lesson or while waiting for parent pickups.

Use these games during transitional moments. While an adult leader is setting up the next activity, have another leader entertain the kids with a quick game.

GAMES

Grab the Finger (pg. 52)   5 min.

Red Light, Green Light (pg. 46)   5 min.

I Spy (pg. 38)   10 min.

Four Corners (pg. 8)   10 min.

Silly Games

Party Planner Guide

Tips:

Have a camera ready to capture these funny, memorable moments. They'll make great photos for a scrapbook or digital slideshow.

There's nothing funnier than having an adult participate in a silly or gross out game! Get in there and really play it up with over the top reactions.

Let the kids pick some of the actions. They often think of the silliest things and will pick things that are silly to them.

GAMES

Seltzer Shoot Out (pg. 59)	10 min.
The Toaster Game (pg. 47)	20 min.
Popcorn (pg. 16)	15 min.
Animal Noises (pg. 9)	10 min.

Icebreaker Games

Party Planner Guide

Tips:

Children's parties and special events can lead to friendships that last a lifetime. Remember to survey the room and ensure each child is involved and having fun. If you sense shyness or a lack of interaction among the group, stop for a moment and use an ice breaker to eliminate some anxiety.

Starting a party with an icebreaker is a great way to calm the nerves. It keeps kids focused on the game and not their anxiety of meeting new people. Once everyone's relaxed, the party will be that much more fun!

GAMES

Name Game (pg. 28)   10 min.

"Have you ever?..." (pg. 54)   15 min.

Continuum (pg. 13)   15 min.

I Didn't Catch Your Name (pg. 44)   10 min.

High Energy Games

Party Planner Guide

Tips:

Active games are a great way to calm down a group of energetic kids. They provide lots of running, shouting, and social interaction. The kids will be so focused on the game, they won't have any time for mischief!

When planning out the event, schedule the active, run around wild games first. It gives an instant sense of excitement to the party and helps calm the kids for quieter games later on. Be sure to have plenty of drinks and snacks on hand after a big, high energy game.

GAMES

Snakes in the Gutter (pg. 23)	20 min.
Lonely Farmer (pg. 6)	30 min.
Relay Races (pg. 34)	15 min.
Capture the Flag (pg. 26)	30 min.

Sleepover Games

Party Planner Guide

Tips:

Since junk food is a major part of any sleepover, have candy or treat prizes for playing each game. Random prizes throughout the game are a good way to keep things exciting and ensure everyone gets a treat.

Near the end of the night, hand out special awards for Silliest Answer, Best Acting, Fastest Time, Most Epic Dance Moves, etc. The kids will get a souvenir to bring home and something to remind them of all the fun they had.

GAMES

Sardines (pg. 37)	45 min.
Bug Hunt (pg. 31)	30 min.
Piggy Wants a Signal (pg. 63)	30 min.
Back to Back (pg. 57)	10 min.

Large Group Games

Party Planner Guide

Tips:

Constant activity is the key to managing a large group of children. Have activities going while children arrive at the event. Throughout the event, always be transitioning from one activity to the next. This keeps the event exciting for the kids and helps minimize disruptions.

Remember to provide incentives for good behavior. Hand out raffle tickets for good listening, helping others, or being the first to line up. Special prizes will encourage the group to keep a good attitude and be respectful to others.

GAMES

Game	Time
Giants, Wizards, and Elves (pg. 39)	15 min.
Red Rover (pg. 41)	20 min.
What Time Is It, Mister Fox? (pg. 29)	15 min.
Two Extremes (pg. 42)	10 min.